Kingdom Rich

God's View on Financial Riches

Sonia O'Brien

© 2021 by *David O'Brien*
ISBN: 978-0-9828843-4-8

All rights reserved. This book is protected by the copyright laws of the United States of America. This book may not be copied or reprinted for commercial gain or profit. The use of quotations or photocopying for personal or group study, or for free distribution without distorting the original work, is permitted and encouraged. Credit and contact information must be included as follows: "Kingdom Rich, BlueDiamondBookhouse.com, Copyright © 2021, used by permission." Other permission may be granted upon request.

Scripture quotations are taken from the following Bible versions:
The Holy Bible, English Standard Version copyright © 2001, 2007, 2011, 2016 by Crossway Books and Bibles, a Publishing Ministry of Good News Publishers. Used by permission. All rights reserved.
The New King James Version. Copyright © 1982 by Thomas Nelson, Inc. Used by permission. All rights reserved
King James Version (KJV), 1611, 1769. Outside of the United Kingdom, the KJV is in the public domain.

Abbreviations are as follows:
NKJ – New King James Version
ESV – English Standard Version
KVJ – King James Version

Blue Diamond Bookhouse

www.BlueDiamondBookhouse.com

Contents

Introduction..vi

1. My Motivation for Writing............................1

2. Three Views on Money..................................3

3. Rich People in the Bible................................5

4. What Is Kingdom Rich?................................11

5. Why Should We be Kingdom Rich?............13

6. How do We Become Kingdom Rich?..........17

7. What Hinders Kingdom Rich?....................29

8. Misconceptions About Money....................33

9. Closing Words..42

Recommended Resources................................43

Introduction

Dear Readers,

Thank you for reading. In this book, I invite you to dig into the Bible—the Word of God—to see what God's view is on financial prosperity. Looking at the truth may change your view on financial riches. If this book provokes or changes your thinking on money, I'd call it a success. It's OK to have new thoughts, and it's great to align our minds with the truth, and just the truth, according to the living, Word of God.

Before reading this book, I encourage you to set aside assumptions about financial riches. Just relax and take a stroll with me in the Scriptures regarding this interesting and important topic.

Before I start, I'd like to thank my heavenly Father for bringing me Biblical truth on wealth through Apostle Charles Ndifon's eye-opening, wisdom and revelations. I thank God for him. I am also thankful to my dear husband for his love and support.

Chapter 1
My Motivation for Writing

Our personal backgrounds and environment influence us greatly on how we view being rich.

Being rich is a relative term. One man's treasure is another man's garbage. So when I talk about being rich, I mean that a person is affluent financially compared to peers in his environment. A rich person in a village obviously may not be considered as rich, as a rich person in New York City.

I grew up in a communist country. My family was not poor or wealthy. Looking back, I never lacked anything. I was well fed, had decent clothes and lived in an apartment with my parents. My parents saved money all their lives. We never had any luxuries by Western standards. I never felt poor, and yet I surely never felt we were rich. The "wisdom" they gave me was to save money and never squander it. "It's good enough to have a stable job, live from paycheck to paycheck and save as much as you can. Spend money to take care of yourself and your family. Be content." I never dreamed of being rich or having my own business, etc.

The bottom line is I grew up without being taught the concept or possibility of being rich. I figured, "Being rich is rich people's portion. It's nice to have nice stuff, but some things are just too nice and you just look at them and admire the rich people that actually enjoy them." Interestingly, in a communist society, people don't have the concept of sharing either. It's noble enough to just take care of your family. Taking care of the poor is the government's job.

After I became a Christian, a brother taught me to give money to the Gospel according to the Bible. As a new believer, I didn't want to, and I had never given money to anybody simply because the concept of giving was too foreign to me! Remember, I was taught that we should take care of ourselves and our families. That was my duty, not taking care of anyone else. In a communist society, you try to get things; you don't really give. Everyone is in survival mode. He shared a Bible verse with me, and I trusted him and started to give. Since then, I have been giving more and more money to the Gospel as my understanding about giving grows.

But back to being rich again. As an adult, until recently, I still never thought I would be rich or should be rich. I figured, "Being rich is not my portion. I should just try to make money and save money with my job and hope for a better life."

Finally, I came across some teaching revealing God's kingdom view on money in the Bible. At first, I was skeptical because it was different from my previous views about money, both as an unbeliever and a believer. This bothered me, and I decided to dig into the Bible and find out the truth for myself. What I discovered was mind boggling and amazing.

I invite you on this journey of finding these truths with me, through this book.

Chapter 2
Three Views on Money

Most people want money and desire to be rich for obvious reasons. In society, it represents status, success, power, and it brings luxury and enjoyment of life. That said, there are various different ways of thinking about money. Here are three common views of different types of people:

Type 1: those who love money.

Money lovers go get money, sit on it and feel, "The more, the better." This view often drives people to excel in life and eventually they do become rich. They want to get money, hold on to as much as possible, for as long as possible, and make some more. Sharing their riches is not on their agenda.

Type 2: those who disdain money.

These people often live in poverty and don't think they can ever get out of it. They don't use their talents or take opportunities to make changes in life. They are either content being poor or wish they were rich. Sometimes they are jealous of rich people, but they don't make any changes or effort, and in some cases are being fed on welfare.

Some people who disdain money live a comfortable life themselves, but, somehow, they are against the concept of being rich. They seem to shun the topic of being wealthy; they don't like to talk about themselves or others being or becoming rich, and yet their life is not uncomfortable. Ironically, they do make efforts to live a comfortable life. This can be a form of self-deception, due to a lack of understanding in this area. Sometimes this is due to religious, traditional views.

Type 3: those who desire to be rich but choose to live a mediocre life.

I was this type. I was OK with living from paycheck to paycheck. I didn't purposefully develop my God-given talents or look for opportunities to advance myself. I made zero effort to gain extra wealth, just hoping life could be better someday. I felt that a rich life was kind of desirable but always far away from me, and not my portion. So I ended up mindlessly going through life, doing my job and admiring others who were rich, but not making any changes for myself or the Kingdom. Passivity, laziness or tunnel-vision can be involved in this view.

Chapter 3
Rich People in the Bible

Is being rich acceptable in God's eyes? Are there any rich among God's people in the Bible? Let's find out.

Example 1 - Abraham:

So Abram went up from Egypt, he and his wife and all that he had, and Lot with him, into the Negeb. 2 Now Abram was very rich in livestock, in silver, and in gold. 3 And he journeyed on from the Negeb as far as Bethel to the place where his tent had been at the beginning, between Bethel and Ai, 4 to the place where he had made an altar at the first. And there Abram called upon the name of the LORD. 5 And Lot, who went with Abram, also had flocks and herds and tents, 6 so that the land could not support both of them dwelling together; for their possessions were so great that they could not dwell together. (Gen 13:1-6)

The Bible says here Abram was very rich in livestock, in silver, and in gold. He was not just rich, but VERY rich. His and Lot's possessions were so great that they couldn't dwell together. Because of this, they had to separate.

The LORD said to Abram, after Lot had separated from him, "Lift up your eyes and look from the place where you are, northward and southward and eastward and westward, 15 for all the land that you see I will give to you and to your offspring forever. 16 I will make your offspring as the dust of the earth, so that if one can count the dust of the earth, your offspring also can be counted. 17 Arise, walk through the length and the breadth of the land, for I will give it to you." (Gen 13: 14-17)

Again, the Lord gave Abram and his offspring ALL the land that he could see, forever. And the Lord commanded him to walk through the length and the breadth of the land. Would you call that rich? Isn't that abundance? Absolutely! God absolutely blesses us in our finances. He wants to and He will. It's one of His ways to show us, His children, that He loves and rewards us. It is a pleasure for any loving father to bless his children financially and see them prosper. It is the same with our Father in heaven.

Example 2 - Isaac:

Now there was a famine in the land, besides the former famine that was in the days of Abraham. And Isaac went to Gerar to Abimelech king of the Philistines. 2 And the LORD appeared to him and said, "Do not go down to Egypt; dwell in the land of which I shall tell you. 3 Sojourn in this land, and I will be with you and will bless you, for to you and to your offspring I will give all these lands, and I will establish the oath that I swore to Abraham your father. (Gen 26:1-3)

To show that the Lord would be with Isaac and bless him, the Lord promised Isaac that He would give him all those lands. Owning lands definitely would make Isaac rich.

And Isaac sowed in that land and reaped in the same year a hundredfold. The LORD blessed him, 13 and the man became rich, and gained more and more until he became very wealthy. 14 He had possessions of flocks and herds and many servants, so that the Philistines envied him. 15 (Now the Philistines had stopped and filled with earth all the wells that his father's servants had dug in the days of Abraham his father.) 16 And Abimelech said to Isaac, "Go away from us, for you are much mightier than we." 17 So Isaac departed from there and encamped in the Valley of Gerar and settled there. (Gen 26: 12-17)

After being blessed by the Lord with those lands, Isaac did become very wealthy. You can see Isaac sowed and reaped a hundredfold in the same year. The Lord blessed him and the man became rich, and he kept gaining wealth until he became VERY wealthy, which caused envy among the Philistines. Imagine a hundredfold increase in your wealth. If you make $30,000 a year, one hundredfold increase would be $3,000,000. Again, wealth is a way the Lord blesses us. He is the same yesterday, today and forever. He blessed people abundantly even beyond our imagination in Bible times; He will do the same for you and me today. Being rich through God's blessing is a godly thing. We'll talk about that more in later chapters.

Let's continue with Isaac:

When Abimelech went to him from Gerar with Ahuzzath his adviser and Phicol the commander of his army, 27 Isaac said to them, "Why have you come to me, seeing that you hate me and have sent me away from you?" 28 They said, "We see plainly that the LORD has been with you. So we said, let there be a sworn pact between us, between you and us, and let us make a covenant with you, 29 that you will do us no harm, just as we have not touched you and have done to you nothing but good and have sent you away in peace. You are now the blessed of the LORD." (Gen 26: 26-29)

From Isaac's wealth and the blessings upon him, Abimelech saw plainly the Lord was with him. It was a sign to him. Being rich as a believer can be a sign to the world that God is with us. When we gain riches the right way, it is appealing to the world. It can attract the world to want to come to know our God, their Creator.

Example 3 – Job:

There was a man in the land of Uz whose name was Job, and that man was blameless and upright, one who feared God and turned away from evil. 2 There were born to him seven sons and three daughters. 3 He possessed 7,000 sheep, 3,000 camels, 500 yoke of oxen, and 500 female donkeys, and very many servants, so that this man was the greatest of all the people of the east.... And the LORD said to Satan, "Have you considered my servant Job, that there is none like him on the earth, a blameless and upright man, who fears God and turns away from evil?" (Job 1:1-3, 8)

Wow! What an honor Job had. He was considered by God to be His blameless and upright servant with none like him. And he was the wealthiest of all the people of the east.

Then Satan answered the LORD and said, "Does Job fear God for no reason? 10 Have you not put a hedge around him and his house and all that he has, on every side? You have blessed the

work of his hands, and his possessions have increased in the land. (Job 1:9)

Satan knew that Job's great wealth was because God had blessed the work of his hands. God was behind Job's prosperity. If God made Bible people prosper then, He will make us prosper today. He is the same yesterday, today and forever.

God allowed Satan to attack Job and his family. Job lost all his wealth and all his sons and daughters.

In all this Job did not sin or charge God with wrong. (Job 1:22)

Job remained blameless from the beginning to the end even when his wife asked him to curse God and die! What happened to Job in the end? Let's look at it:

And the LORD restored the fortunes of Job, when he had prayed for his friends. And the LORD gave Job twice as much as he had before. 11 Then came to him all his brothers and sisters and all who had known him before, and ate bread with him in his house. And they showed him sympathy and comforted him for all the evil that the LORD had brought upon him. And each of them gave him a piece of money and a ring of gold. 12 And the LORD blessed the latter days of Job more than his beginning. And he had 14,000 sheep, 6,000 camels, 1,000 yoke of oxen, and 1,000 female donkeys. 13 He had also seven sons and three daughters. 14 And he called the name of the first daughter Jemimah, and the name of the second Keziah, and the name of the third Keren-happuch. 15 And in all the land there were no women so beautiful as Job's daughters. And their father gave them an inheritance among their brothers. 16 And after this Job lived 140 years, and saw his sons, and his sons' sons, four generations. 17 And Job died, an old man, and full of days. (Job 42:10-17)

This is such an amazing story. In verse 12, it says the Lord blessed the latter days of Job more than his beginning and made him richer. Can you imagine what a wonderful and enjoyable life Job had in his latter days because of God's blessings? Wow, our God is an amazing blesser.

Example 4 – Jacob:

Now Jacob heard that the sons of Laban were saying, "Jacob has taken all that was our father's, and from what was our father's he has gained all this wealth.... Thus God has taken away the livestock of your father and given them to me. (Gen 31:1, 9)

Again, God was the one who gave Jacob livestock and made him gain wealth. When Jacob saw his brother Esau and offered him gifts, Esau refused him. But the Word says:

But Esau said, "I have enough, my brother; keep what you have for yourself." 10 Jacob said, "No, please, if I have found favor in your sight, then accept my present from my hand. For I have seen your face, which is like seeing the face of God, and you have accepted me. 11 Please accept my blessing that is brought to you, because God has dealt graciously with me, and because I have enough." Thus he urged him, and he took it. (Gen 33:9-11)

God dealt graciously with Jacob, so he had enough. His abundance was all because of God.

Example 5 – Solomon:

Solomon the son of David established himself in his kingdom, and the LORD his God was with him and made him exceedingly great.... In that night God appeared to Solomon, and said to him, "Ask what I shall give you." 8 And Solomon said to God, "You have shown great and steadfast love to David my father, and have made me king in his place. 9 O LORD God, let your word to David my father be now fulfilled, for you have made me king over a people as numerous as the dust of the earth. 10 Give me now wisdom and knowledge to go out and come in before this people, for who can govern this people of yours, which is so great?" 11 God answered Solomon, "Because this was in your heart, and you have not asked for possessions, wealth, honor, or the life of those who hate you, and have not even asked for long life, but have asked for wisdom and knowledge for yourself that you may govern my people over whom I have made you king, 12 wisdom and knowledge are granted to you. I will also give you riches,

possessions, and honor, such as none of the kings had who were before you, and none after you shall have the like." (2Ch 1:1, 7-12)

Because Solomon was asking for wisdom and knowledge to govern his people, which pleased God, in return, He rewarded him by also giving him riches, possessions, and honor besides giving him knowledge and wisdom. The amount God gave him was so great, that no kings before or after him had the like. Again, God loves to bless and reward people with riches, possessions and honor.

Chapter 4
What Is Kingdom Rich?

In this book, when I say rich, I mean *kingdom rich*—a type of rich that God initiates and sustains. It is a characteristic of belonging to God's kingdom as His children. We become kingdom rich for God. That's why it's called "kingdom rich." It's not rich by mere worldly standards. I'll explain more as you read along.

From that time Jesus began to preach, saying, "Repent, for the kingdom of heaven is at hand." (Matthew 4:17)

And he went throughout all Galilee, teaching in their synagogues and proclaiming the gospel of the kingdom and healing every disease and every affliction among the people. (Matthew 4:23)

The gospel Jesus was proclaiming is called the gospel of the kingdom. He has a kingdom. He is the King of kings. He rules. As we enter into His kingdom by believing in Him, we rule with Him also. The gospel of the kingdom is not a religion. We are involved in a kingdom operation. Everything we do should be with a kingdom mentality, more precisely, a kingdom identity. This means we do what Jesus did—operating as kings in Christ Jesus and ruling in this life—for the sole purpose of bringing God's kingdom down to earth as in heaven. We are called sons and daughters of the mighty God. We belong to kingdom royalty, and we are kings—nothing less.

Now, as we still have time to live on this earth to fulfill our God-given destinies before Jesus returns, we ought to rule. Ruling on earth under Jesus, the head, is our responsibility. That's why we were given authority to tread on serpents and scorpions, and over all the power of the enemy, and nothing shall hurt us. (Luke 10:19) We rule in all circumstances through Jesus.

In fact, the word "church" in the Bible means "ruling assembly." (I recommend my husband's book, "Return to Acts Christianity," for more detail on this subject). We are the church. We are the ruling assembly. We are not a crowd of churchgoers or spectators of any sort.

We are soldiers on this earth dispatched from Heaven to carry out a special mission on this earth. What's the special mission? It is the great commission assigned to each one of us by our King, Jesus on the day we chose to become his disciples. Everybody has a vital part to play in this mission. No one can be replaced.

And Jesus came and said to them, "All authority in heaven and on earth has been given to me. 19 Go therefore and make disciples of all nations, baptizing them in the name of the Father and of the Son and of the Holy Spirit, 20 teaching them to observe all that I have commanded you. And behold, I am with you always, to the end of the age." (Matthew 28: 18-20)

We bring heaven to earth. When people see us, they see Jesus in us. When we touch them, they are touched by Jesus. When we encounter an adverse situation, it is reversed for good. We always bring good news. We always have the solution. We are called to be the light; the light is in us and shines through us. We are destined to be solution givers. We are obligated to bring heaven to earth. The great commission stated in Matthew 28:18-20 is the focus of everything we do. It is the mission statement of the Kingdom of Jesus Christ. If we can understand it, we can then have the kingdom mentality. We can walk into our kingdom identity—our true identity. With this in mind, we can talk about kingdom rich.

Kingdom rich is to be rich God's way for the purpose of bringing God's kingdom to earth, which is accomplishing the great commission. This is every believer's obligation and privilege.

Chapter 5
Why Should We be Kingdom Rich?

Why should we be kingdom rich? The reason is provided by the Word of God throughout the Bible.

Can you imagine a person of royalty being poor? Maybe some over-the-hill kingdom on earth, but not a chance in God's kingdom. In heaven, the flooring is made of gold. Our Father owns everything in heaven and on earth. And in heaven, nothing good is lacking. If our heavenly Father is rich, as his inheritors, we are too.

Our Father called us to bring heaven to earth. Jesus prayed this in Matthew 6:10: "Your kingdom come, your will be done, on earth as it is in heaven." It is our calling to bring heaven to earth, including riches.

Beloved, I wish above all things that thou mayest prosper and be in health, even as thy soul prospereth. (3 John 1:2, KJV)

When you look at this verse in the Greek context, the word "above" here actually should've been translated, "concerning." In other words, John was saying: beloved, I wish concerning all things, you may prosper and be in health, even as your soul prospers.

We see this verse a lot when people talk about healing. According to this verse, God wants us to prosper concerning ALL things. That means our finances are included, and they should prosper.

Deuteronomy 28:1-14 records blessings for obedience:

"And if you faithfully obey the voice of the LORD your God, being careful to do all his commandments that I command you today, the LORD your God will set you high above all the nations of the earth. 2 And all these blessings shall come upon you and overtake you, if you obey the voice of the LORD your God. 3 Blessed shall you be in the city, and blessed shall you be in the field. 4 Blessed shall be the fruit of your womb and the fruit of your ground and the fruit of your cattle, the increase of your

herds and the young of your flock. 5 Blessed shall be your basket and your kneading bowl. 6 Blessed shall you be when you come in, and blessed shall you be when you go out. 7 "The LORD will cause your enemies who rise against you to be defeated before you. They shall come out against you one way and flee before you seven ways. 8 The LORD will command the blessing on you in your barns and in all that you undertake. And he will bless you in the land that the LORD your God is giving you. 9 The LORD will establish you as a people holy to himself, as he has sworn to you, if you keep the commandments of the LORD your God and walk in his ways. 10 And all the peoples of the earth shall see that you are called by the name of the LORD, and they shall be afraid of you. 11 And the LORD will make you abound in prosperity, in the fruit of your womb and in the fruit of your livestock and in the fruit of your ground, within the land that the LORD swore to your fathers to give you. 12 The LORD will open to you his good treasury, the heavens, to give the rain to your land in its season and to bless all the work of your hands. And you shall lend to many nations, but you shall not borrow. 13 And the LORD will make you the head and not the tail, and you shall only go up and not down, if you obey the commandments of the LORD your God, which I command you today, being careful to do them, 14 and if you do not turn aside from any of the words that I command you today, to the right hand or to the left, to go after other gods to serve them."

From these verses we can see that when we obey God:
- Verse 3: we shall be blessed in the city; we shall be blessed in the field.
- Verse 4: The Lord blesses the fruit of your ground, the fruit of your cattle and increases your herds.
- Verse 5: The Lord blesses your basket and your kneading bowl.
- Verse 8: The Lord will command the blessing on you in your barns and in all that you undertake. And He will bless you in the land.
- Verse 11: The Lord will make you abound in prosperity, in the fruit of your ground, within the land that the LORD swore to your fathers to give you.
- Verse 12: The Lord will open to you His good treasury, and bless all the work of your hands. You shall lend to many nations, but you

shall not borrow.

We are the head, not the tail, in every aspect our lives, absolutely including our finances.

Jesus is sitting at the right hand of the throne. He has done His part. According to His command, now it's our turn to finish the remaining work, until he returns. God needs us to do our part, then He can do His part. If we don't move, He can't move. Authority is given to us. The responsibility of the great commission falls on us. We need to represent Jesus wherever we go, in everything we do.

Now when Jesus heard this, he withdrew from there in a boat to a desolate place by himself. But when the crowds heard it, they followed him on foot from the towns. 14 When he went ashore he saw a great crowd, and he had compassion on them and healed their sick. 15 Now when it was evening, the disciples came to him and said, "This is a desolate place, and the day is now over; send the crowds away to go into the villages and buy food for themselves." 16 But Jesus said, "They need not go away; you give them something to eat." 17 They said to him, "We have only five loaves here and two fish." 18 And he said, "Bring them here to me." 19 Then he ordered the crowds to sit down on the grass, and taking the five loaves and the two fish, he looked up to heaven and said a blessing. Then he broke the loaves and gave them to the disciples, and the disciples gave them to the crowds. 20 And they all ate and were satisfied. And they took up twelve baskets full of the broken pieces left over. 21 And those who ate were about five thousand men, besides women and children. (Matt 14: 13-21)

There is more than one example of Jesus feeding a big crowd. This is one of them. We should be able to produce abundance. We should be able to bless people in need by meeting their basic needs. That's how God is. He cares. He is full of compassion. He is more than enough. He is not a barely-get-by type of God. He is not stingy. He is a giver, and he always looks for someone to bless, because He is love.

We need to be kingdom rich to reflect Him. We need to be kingdom rich to complete the great commission. We need to be kingdom rich to be in line with His will for us. We need to be kingdom rich to reflect our Father. We need to be kingdom rich to bring Him glory. It is God's will for us to be kingdom rich.

Chapter 6
How do We Become Kingdom Rich?

First, kingdom rich originates with God:

Let's look at two verses:

For you know the grace of our Lord Jesus Christ, that though he was rich, yet for your sake he became poor, so that you by his poverty might become rich. (2Cor 8:9)

Beloved, I pray that you may prosper in all things and be in health, just as your soul prospers. (3Jn 1:2 NKJ)

I chose the New King James version for this second verse because it accurately translates the word for "prosper." The Greek word "euodoo" was used in this verse, which means "prosper."

Kingdom rich is based on the truth that for our sake, Jesus died on the cross and rose again after three days, so that we can trade our poverty with His riches. Because of His sacrifice, by His initiative, kingdom rich is available to us. Kingdom rich is not produced by our own ability, smartness, hard work, etc. It originates from God himself. That's also why John was able to say we may prosper in all things. "All" means all, including our finances, physical bodies, relationships, etc. If Jesus didn't pay the price for us, we couldn't be delivered out of our own poverty or receive physical healings or other miracles. Thank God that it is His will for us to be kingdom rich.

Second, to become kingdom rich, seek the kingdom of God first:

Therefore I tell you, do not be anxious about your life, what you will eat or what you will drink, nor about your body, what you will put on. Is not life more than food, and the body more than clothing? 26 Look at the birds of the air: they neither sow nor reap nor gather into barns, and yet your heavenly Father feeds them. Are you not of more value than they? 27 And which of you by being anxious can add a single hour to his span of life? 28 And

why are you anxious about clothing? Consider the lilies of the field, how they grow: they neither toil nor spin, 29 yet I tell you, even Solomon in all his glory was not arrayed like one of these.
30 But if God so clothes the grass of the field, which today is alive and tomorrow is thrown into the oven, will he not much more clothe you, O you of little faith? 31 Therefore do not be anxious, saying, 'What shall we eat?' or 'What shall we drink?' or 'What shall we wear?' 32 For the Gentiles seek after all these things, and your heavenly Father knows that you need them all. 33 But seek first the kingdom of God and his righteousness, and all these things will be added to you. (Matt 6:25-33)

Everyone in the world knows and desires to purse a better life through chasing money, going to school, finding a job, climbing a company ladder, etc. Chasing after money is in their DNA. They know it and do it without a second thought. For us believers, we need to choose what the Word says.

First of all, we are not allowed to worry about what to eat and what to wear. We are commanded to not worry about tomorrow. The Word says our heavenly Father knows all that we need. In fact, He knows even before we ask Him about anything. We are instructed to seek the kingdom of God and His righteousness first, "and all these things will be added to you." In other words, they will chase after us! This includes physical riches and all other needs. Thank God for this promise. We don't have to strive on our own to take care of ourselves anymore. We have a heavenly Father who already promised to take care of us. We are in good, good hands if we allow Him to help us in this way.

At the same time, we do have an something to do in order for God to move and take care of us. Verse 33: we seek first the kingdom of God. As we seek first the kingdom of God, finding out His will for us and doing what He calls us to do, with obedience and faithfulness, He will provide for us. Seeking first the kingdom of God is the only right foundation for becoming kingdom rich. On this foundation, we will be able to please God. When God is pleased with us, He will never be hesitant to bless us financially. When we make this right move, He will move next, to give us power and wisdom to be kingdom rich.

Abraham was obedient to God as God called him to leave his family for a foreign land. He was told to sacrifice his only son to God. He obeyed God's commands again and again without any doubt or resistance. This is his example of seeking first the kingdom of God and His righteousness. Abraham's obedience and faithfulness pleased God and that made God want to bless him, and He eventually made him extremely rich. This is just one example in the Bible. There are so many others. They have the same pattern. They first seek the kingdom of God and His righteousness. They pleased God first. Then God decided to make them rich. That's what I call kingdom rich. Abraham is our spiritual father. As his offspring, we inherit his faith and blessings. We ought to imitate his faith. Shouldn't we imitate how he pleased God and became kingdom rich also? To me, the answer is absolutely yes!

When we obey God and are in His will, this is what He'll do for us:

The LORD will command the blessing on you in your barns and in all that you undertake. And he will bless you in the land that the LORD your God is giving you. (Deut 28:8)

Third, God is the one who gives us power to become kingdom rich:

You shall remember the LORD your God, for it is he who gives you power to get wealth, that he may confirm his covenant that he swore to your fathers, as it is this day. (Deut 8:18)

When Moses gave instructions from God to Israel, he told them that it is the Lord their God who gave them power to get wealth. If the Lord didn't bless them, if He didn't agree with what they did and wasn't on their side, they could not have had that power to gain wealth.

When it comes to gaining kingdom riches, we need to understand that they never come from our own smartness, intelligence or hard work. This doesn't mean we don't use our talents or work hard. It means we need to recognize that when we are on the path of life, He will give us power to gain kingdom riches. We can never go out on our own and try to figure things out while setting God aside and relying on our own understanding.

Joseph in the Bible was sold by his brothers into slavery in Egypt.

What started as a tragedy but had a powerful and beautiful ending for his family and for nations. Thank God the Bible is true, and we can learn from men and women who lived real lives. They experienced deep pain and joy in life. When Joseph was in Egypt, Genesis 39:2 says:

The LORD was with Joseph, and he became a successful man, and he was in the house of his Egyptian master. 3 His master saw that the LORD was with him and that the LORD caused all that he did to succeed in his hands. 4 So Joseph found favor in his sight and attended him, and he made him overseer of his house and put him in charge of all that he had. 5 From the time that he made him overseer in his house and over all that he had, the LORD blessed the Egyptian's house for Joseph's sake; the blessing of the LORD was on all that he had, in house and field. (Gen 39:2)

The Lord was with Joseph—that's what made him successful! That was the root reason for his success. I'm sure Joseph was a hard worker with good traits and work ethics, but without the Lord, he couldn't make it to the top in his master's house.

When we tune into God and rely on Him, He will provide us with great ideas and inspiration, and also divine connections. He will endow us with favor, provide us with resources, knowledge and wisdom.

When things were looking really good for Joseph, he faced another test—his master's wife cast her eyes on him, tempted him and falsely accused him. Because he was innocent and right with the Lord, even when he was put in prison, the Lord was with him.

But the LORD was with Joseph and showed him steadfast love and gave him favor in the sight of the keeper of the prison. 22 And the keeper of the prison put Joseph in charge of all the prisoners who were in the prison. Whatever was done there, he was the one who did it. 23 The keeper of the prison paid no attention to anything that was in Joseph's charge, because the LORD was with him. And whatever he did, the LORD made it succeed. (Gen 39:21-23)

Whatever he did, the Lord made succeed! God gives us power to gain success wherever we go, even in the lowest place such as a prison, as long as we are right with Him.

In Genesis 40, we read that later the Lord gave Joseph wisdom and understanding to interpret two prisoners' dreams. One of them was a cupbearer to the king. After he got out of the prison, he didn't keep his promise to help Joseph. So Joseph had to stay in prison another two years. After that, he had another chance to interpret a dream of Pharaoh's, when no one else in Egypt could. Not only did God give Joseph the ability to interpret his dream, He also gave him a solution to a potential disaster due to a famine. And this was Pharaoh's response:

And Pharaoh said to his servants, "Can we find a man like this, in whom is the Spirit of God?" 39 Then Pharaoh said to Joseph, "Since God has shown you all this, there is none so discerning and wise as you are. 40 You shall be over my house, and all my people shall order themselves as you command. Only as regards the throne will I be greater than you." 41 And Pharaoh said to Joseph, "See, I have set you over all the land of Egypt." 42 Then Pharaoh took his signet ring from his hand and put it on Joseph's hand, and clothed him in garments of fine linen and put a gold chain about his neck. 43 And he made him ride in his second chariot. And they called out before him, "Bow the knee!" Thus he set him over all the land of Egypt. 44 Moreover, Pharaoh said to Joseph, "I am Pharaoh, and without your consent no one shall lift up hand or foot in all the land of Egypt." (Gen 41:38-44)

Once again, Joseph rose from ashes all the way to the top because the Lord gave him power to reach complete success. Joseph's success with Pharaoh was not only pivotal for his family and Egypt, but also for the rest of human history. And his prosperity and success in Egypt was not accidental. God had a good plan for his life from the very beginning, and he did not miss it because he was obedient and faithful to God regardless of his circumstances.

He didn't go up and down. He stayed stable and trusted God every single step. (Thank you God that you give us power to gain wealth and success for your kingdom's sake). He is the same yesterday, today and tomorrow. He did that for Joseph; He will do it for you and me today. I believe He needs more Josephs in today's time to accomplish His will on earth. He's waiting to see who is qualified and available to be given power for wealth and success. Raise your hand and let God know you're willing to be a Joseph and to be used by Him today.

Fourth, now that we know what it is and why we should be kingdom rich, what do we do next?

The answer is to take action. Be kingdom rich! It's like any other command in the Bible—once we learn it, we need to act on it. We can't just walk away from truth, or we'll never change. Kingdom rich is the same. When we understand the need to be kingdom rich, we must go after it. Everyone was born with God's image and has been given talents and gifts. We need to discover and use them to the fullest. Otherwise we'd be wasting what was put in us, and that would sadden our Father's heart.

"For it will be like a man going on a journey, who called his servants and entrusted to them his property. 15 To one he gave five talents[1], to another two, to another one, to each according to his ability. Then he went away. 16 He who had received the five talents went at once and traded with them, and he made five talents more. 17 So also he who had the two talents made two talents more. 18 But he who had received the one talent went and dug in the ground and hid his master's money. 19 Now after a long time the master of those servants came and settled accounts with them. 20 And he who had received the five talents came forward, bringing five talents more, saying, 'Master, you delivered to me five talents; here, I have made five talents more.' 21 His master said to him, 'Well done, good and faithful servant. You have been faithful over a little; I will set you over much. Enter into the joy of your master.' 22 And he also who had the two talents came forward, saying, 'Master, you delivered to me two talents; here, I have made two talents more.' 23 His master said to him, 'Well done, good and faithful servant. You have been

---

[1] "A *talent* was a monetary unit worth about twenty years' wages for a laborer" (The Holy Bible, English Standard Version copyright © 2001, 2007, 2011, 2016 by Crossway Books and Bibles, a Publishing Ministry of Good News Publishers. Used by permission. All rights reserved). It was used to represent our abilities and "talents."

faithful over a little; I will set you over much. Enter into the joy of your master.' 24 He also who had received the one talent came forward, saying, 'Master, I knew you to be a hard man, reaping where you did not sow, and gathering where you scattered no seed, 25 so I was afraid, and I went and hid your talent in the ground. Here, you have what is yours.' 26 But his master answered him, 'You wicked and slothful servant! You knew that I reap where I have not sown and gather where I scattered no seed? 27 Then you ought to have invested my money with the bankers, and at my coming I should have received what was my own with interest. 28 So take the talent from him and give it to him who has the ten talents. 29 For to everyone who has will more be given, and he will have an abundance. But from the one who has not, even what he has will be taken away. 30 And cast the worthless servant into the outer darkness. In that place there will be weeping and gnashing of teeth.' (Matt 25: 14-30)

Everyone was created in God's image. Everyone has talents and gifts. As believers, we need to proactively discover what's in us, develop it and use it for God's kingdom and His purpose for our lives. God has a great plan for each one of us. Satan always tries to blind us from seeing what God has for us and distract us from the right path, with lies. We need to renew our minds with the Word of God and guard our hearts and minds to make sure they're always in line with the truth. This will ensure we find God's will for us and discover godly desires God has put in us. Then we need to proactively pursue those things, meaning we must take action and be diligent.

Some people never come to the point of knowing what God has for them. They don't know what they really want to do. Some people have discovered what they are called to do and the desires God has put in them. But they don't pursue it proactively. In other words, they put no effort and make no sacrifice to make their dreams come true. In the end they live in regret and an unfulfilled life. If you are not called to be a lawyer, even if you became the most successful lawyer, you wouldn't feel satisfied or fulfilled until you turn around and choose God's path, designed for you before the foundation of the earth.

So I encourage you to take time to find out what God called you to do. A lot of times His will for us matches the deep desires in our hearts.

He will develop us to be the best we can be, to do the job He has for us. When you are on the right path, everything will fall into its place. Connections will be made; resources will be provided; favor will be bestowed, and doors will open. But we have to make the move proactively. For example, if you have the desire to create children's books, take small steps to move toward that dream by taking a drawing class and learn how to write stories. Don't just talk the talk. Be the servant who was given 5000 talents; made 5000 more and was rewarded more. God doesn't like to waste our talents. Use what's been given to us in the most effective way, to the fullest extent. Let me end this point with a wonderful verse in Proverbs 21:29:

Do you see a man skillful in his work? He will stand before kings; he will not stand before obscure men. (Proverbs 21:29)

Dream big! Live your dream, and make our Father glad and proud.

Fifth, be diligent to be kingdom rich:

God makes a move. Then it's our turn to make a move. Then God makes the next move. Then it's our turn to respond. This is how it works in the kingdom of God. He can't do our part. He gave us freedom to choose what we want to do. He watches and sees if we will be obedient and faithful. If we are, blessing follows. Being kingdom rich is the same. We have a part to play. If we don't make the proper moves, God can't make the next moves. One requirement is to be diligent. Let's look at Bible verses about diligence:

A slack hand causes poverty, but the hand of the diligent makes rich. 5 He who gathers in summer is a prudent son, but he who sleeps in harvest is a son who brings shame. (Proverbs 10:4-5)

Being diligent is being prudent. The word "prudent" means "shrewd" (in the positive sense). Being diligent is being shrewd. The hand of the diligent makes rich.

The hand of the diligent will rule, while the slothful will be put to forced labor. (Proverbs 12:24)

We are called to be the head, not the tail. We are God's ruling assembly. We are called to rule. Therefore, we ought to be diligent.

Whoever is slothful will not roast his game, but the diligent man will get precious wealth. (Proverbs 12:27)

Wealth doesn't automatically fall into our laps. It goes to the diligent man.

The soul of the sluggard craves and gets nothing, while the soul of the diligent is richly supplied. (Proverbs 13:4)

The soul of the diligent is richly supplied. We should lack nothing good. If you want no lack, be diligent.

The plans of the diligent lead surely to abundance, but everyone who is hasty comes only to poverty. (Proverbs 21:5)

The plans of the diligent lead to abundance. Jesus came to give us life, life of abundance. It's God's will for us to have abundance. It's right for us to be diligent.

Being diligent is greatly valued by God, and it's a condition for being kingdom rich. Be diligent to seek God's will. Be diligent to develop and use skills to do what God called you to do. Let's finish this point with this:

Whoever works his land will have plenty of bread, but he who follows worthless pursuits will have plenty of poverty. (Proverbs 28:19)

Sixth, being generous and ready to share is another important condition for being kingdom rich.

Let's look at some verses:

Whoever has a bountiful eye will be blessed, for he shares his bread with the poor. (Proverbs 22:9)

When we consider and take care of the poor, we will be blessed.

Whoever multiplies his wealth by interest and profit gathers it for him who is generous to the poor. (Proverbs 28:8)

Whoever is generous to the poor will gain wealth labored for and produced by the wicked.

A stingy man hastens after wealth and does not know that poverty will come upon him. (Proverbs 28:22)

One can be stingy, no matter how much money he has. The more one wants to hold on to his money, the less money he will have.

Whoever gives to the poor will not want, but he who hides his eyes will get many a curse. (Proverbs 28:27)

Giving to the poor makes us have no want, no lack!

The desire of the sluggard kills him, for his hands refuse to labor. 26 All day long he craves and craves, but the righteous gives and does not hold back. (Proverbs 21:25-26)

The righteous gives. The righteous knows the Father's heart. He does what makes the Father glad—giving to the poor and taking care of them.

As for the rich in this present age, charge them not to be haughty, nor to set their hopes on the uncertainty of riches, but on God, who richly provides us with everything to enjoy. 18 They are to do good, to be rich in good works, to be generous and ready to share, 19 thus storing up treasure for themselves as a good foundation for the future, so that they may take hold of that which is truly life. (1Timothy 6:17-18)

Paul instructed people here to be generous and ready to share. When we share with others financially, we are storing up treasure for ourselves as a good foundation for the future.

Religion that is pure and undefiled before God the Father is this: to visit orphans and widows in their affliction, and to keep oneself unstained from the world. (James 1:27)

To be kingdom rich is not for our own sake. It's for God's kingdom. One of the reasons to be kingdom rich is to help take care of orphans and widows in their affliction.

Now the full number of those who believed were of one heart and soul, and no one said that any of the things that belonged to him was his own, but they had everything in common. 33 And with great power the apostles were giving their testimony to the resurrection of the Lord Jesus, and great grace was upon them all. 34 There was not a needy person among them, for as many as were owners of lands or houses sold them and brought the proceeds of what was sold 35 and laid it at the apostles' feet, and it was distributed to each as any had need. 36 Thus Joseph, who was also called by the apostles Barnabas (which means son of encouragement), a Levite, a native of Cyprus, 37 sold a field that belonged to him and brought the money and laid it at the apostles' feet. (Acts 4:32-37)

These verses perfectly depict how kingdom rich works. Among those early believers, there were many land and house owners. They were rich and generous. They had the kingdom rich concept, so they cared about our Father's business. That's why they were able to sell their possessions and lay it at the apostles' feet. In the end, there was not a needy person among them. That is noble, glorious and godly!

In summary, it's very important for us to give financially. Giving is Biblical. We give according to what we have. Sometimes we give even beyond what we have, by the Holy Spirit. We give willingly out of a glad heart. Giving is more blessed than receiving. This way there won't be a needy person among us, as in Acts 4:34 above.

We give to the poor. We need to take care of orphans and widows, also persecuted believers and their families.

We give to people who nurture and feed us spiritually.

Let the one who is taught the word share all good things with the one who teaches. (Galatians 6:6)

We need to share all good things with the one who teaches us. This is a

Bible command. Nowadays there is a lot of "free" teachings we have access to on the internet. But nothing is really free for the one who put the teachings on the internet. And teachers undergo other costs also, to bring the Word of God to us. We need to be honest and upright in this area.

We need to support the Gospel financially, so the Gospel can be preached to all nations. As commanded in Matthew:

And this gospel of the kingdom will be proclaimed throughout the whole world as a testimony to all nations, and then the end will come. (Matt 24:14)

That is the whole purpose of kingdom rich.

Chapter 7
What Hinders Kingdom Rich?

In this chapter we are going to talk about what things are not kingdom rich, so that we can have a clearer understanding of kingdom rich from the Bible.

First, oppressing the poor:

Whoever oppresses the poor to increase his own wealth, or gives to the rich, will only come to poverty. (Proverbs 22:16)

Do not rob the poor, because he is poor, or crush the afflicted at the gate, 23 for the LORD will plead their cause and rob of life those who rob them. (Proverbs 22:22-23)

Wealth increased by oppressing the poor is not kingdom rich. The consequences of oppressing and robbing the poor are poverty and the Lord will rob of life those who rob the poor.

Second, greed:

Whoever multiplies his wealth by interest and profit gathers it for him who is generous to the poor. (Proverbs 28:8)

A greedy man stirs up strife, but the one who trusts in the LORD will be enriched. (Proverbs: 28:25)

Kingdom rich originates with God and is sustained by obeying God and being right with Him. If we get rich by greed, the wealth won't last long. It will actually go to the ones who are generous to the poor.

Third, being hasty:

A faithful man will abound with blessings, but whoever hastens to be rich will not go unpunished. (Proverbs 28:20)

An inheritance gained hastily in the beginning will not be blessed

in the end. (Proverbs 20:21)

The plans of the diligent lead surely to abundance, but everyone who is hasty comes only to poverty. (Proverbs 21:5)

As we discussed before, kingdom rich originates from God. God is never in a hurry doing anything. He is full of peace. His timing is perfect. If we hasten to become rich without God's initiative and the Holy Spirit's council, the end will be disaster, and we will not go unpunished. This is trusting oneself instead of God.

Fourth, boasting in one's riches:

Thus says the LORD: "Let not the wise man boast in his wisdom, let not the mighty man boast in his might, let not the rich man boast in his riches, 24 but let him who boasts boast in this, that he understands and knows me, that I am the LORD who practices steadfast love, justice, and righteousness in the earth. For in these things I delight, declares the LORD." (Jeremiah 9:23)

When someone is kingdom rich, it has nothing to do with his own ability. It is because God blessed and prospered him for being in His will. So if someone turns around and boasts in his riches, he is completely delusional. And the end of trusting money and oneself is pure destruction.

Fifth, serving two masters:

No one can serve two masters, for either he will hate the one and love the other, or he will be devoted to the one and despise the other. You cannot serve God and money. (Matthew: 6:24:24)

When we are in God's will, we don't pursue money. Money, resources and connections follow us when we are on the right path of God. He will open the right doors and shut wrong ones. We don't strive to be rich. Instead, we relax, flow with God, see what God has for us and let the Holy Spirit be our driver. We let Him lead us where He wants us to go. We have complete submission to God's will at all costs. When we seek first the kingdom of God, all other things will be added to us. All things we need, will chase us. God will be able to be the one who provides for us. We will prosper.

But if the Holy Spirit is not in the driver's seat, if we pursue money for selfish purposes, with a lukewarm attitude toward serving God, things won't work out the way God wants for us. If it's not God's way, it won't be the best way for our lives.

Sixth, being lazy:

The sluggard does not plow in the autumn; he will seek at harvest and have nothing. (Proverbs: 20:4)

Love not sleep, lest you come to poverty; open your eyes, and you will have plenty of bread. (Proverbs 20:13)

The desire of the sluggard kills him, for his hands refuse to labor. 26 All day long he craves and craves, but the righteous gives and does not hold back. (Proverbs 21:25-26)

Prosperity—having plenty and abundance—is a good thing! But if we are lazy, not proactive in developing our skills and talents, not using them for God's kingdom-purposes, we will stay ordinary or even below average. We won't be rich. To be kingdom rich, we have an important part to play. We need to makes moves, just like in receiving the free salvation gift and healing from God. God already promised and made the move; if we don't move, He will not do anything for us. Lazy ones receive nothing.

Seventh, dishonesty:

Unequal weights are an abomination to the LORD, and false scales are not good. (Proverbs 20:23)

Bread gained by deceit is sweet to a man, but afterward his mouth will be full of gravel. (Proverbs 20:17)

God hates evil, crookedness and dishonesty. Unequal weights are an abomination to the Lord. How terrible would it be to have a mouthful of gravel after you think you've had sweet bread?

Eighth, setting hope on riches:

As for the rich in this present age, charge them not to be haughty, nor to set their hopes on the uncertainty of riches, but on God, who richly provides us with everything to enjoy. (1Timothy 6:17)

Relying on riches is a foolish thing. The moment we do that, we fall into the trap of the love of money, which is a root of all evil. If money becomes an idol to us, it will lead us to destruction. This is not the purpose of kingdom rich.

Ninth, loving pleasure:

Whoever loves pleasure will be a poor man; he who loves wine and oil will not be rich. (Proverbs 21:17)

It is clear here that one who loves pleasure will be a poor man. The purpose of kingdom rich is for God's kingdom and the great commission. God gives us all things to enjoy. But kingdom rich is not primarily for our own pleasure.

Chapter 8
Misconceptions About Money

Misconception 1: having money is a bad thing, and I don't need much money in life.

Some people think having money is a bad thing for a believer—to them it's almost despicable to be rich. Others may not be that extreme. They think, "I don't have big needs in life. I am fine not having a lot." These two views both miss the big picture. Being kingdom rich is not about yourself and your needs. Being kingdom rich is being kingdom-oriented. It's for the kingdom's sake. Our becoming rich is not because we lust for a luxurious life. It's because it is God's desire for us to be rich.

For you know the grace of our Lord Jesus Christ, that though he was rich, yet for your sake he became poor, so that you by his poverty might become rich. (2 Corinthians 8:9)

Jesus paid the price on the cross for us, so we can trade our poverty with His richness. If being kingdom rich is a bad thing, why don't we all strive for poverty? No one does that.

If a rich man gives money to the Gospel, regardless of if he is a believer or not, we all would rejoice and say, "Praise the Lord." We think it's a good thing to fund the Gospel, right? But why can't we be the one writing the check to make someone's life better? Why do we always wait for someone else to do it? Aren't we supposed to be the head, not the tail? Aren't we destined by God to lead and rule as the ruling assembly on earth? Aren't we supposed to be like Jesus feeding multitudes of people?

As for the rich in this present age, charge them not to be haughty, nor to set their hopes on the uncertainty of riches, but on God, who richly provides us with everything to enjoy. (1 Timothy 6:17)

As a good, good Father, God provides us with everything to enjoy. Living in poverty is not enjoyable. It's the opposite of God's will. You can enjoy everything richly provided by God without setting your hope on the uncertainty of riches. Bible heroes did that. We can too.

"Truly, truly, I say to you, whoever believes in me will also do the works that I do; and greater works than these will he do, because I am going to the Father. (John 14:12)

We are supposed to be His hands and feet. We are supposed to do greater works than he did.

People often quote the following verse to say that we need to be content with little and we are not supposed to be rich.

But godliness with contentment is great gain, 7 for we brought nothing into the world, and we cannot take anything out of the world. 8 But if we have food and clothing, with these we will be content. 9 But those who desire to be rich fall into temptation, into a snare, into many senseless and harmful desires that plunge people into ruin and destruction. 10 For the love of money is a root of all kinds of evils. It is through this craving that some have wandered away from the faith and pierced themselves with many pangs. 11 But as for you, O man of God, flee these things. Pursue righteousness, godliness, faith, love, steadfastness, gentleness. (1 (Timothy 6: 6-10)

When reading the Bible, we need to consider the big picture behind any truth, and read and understand it in context. Otherwise truth can be twisted and misused to mislead people. In these verses, Paul said in verse 8 that we will be content if we have food and clothing. People use this verse to say we shouldn't be rich, that we shouldn't have more than food and clothing.

In actual fact, Paul never said we should not have more than food and clothing. He said we will be content if we have food and clothing. Being content has nothing to do with having little or much. A person can be greedy and discontent regardless of how much he owns. Paul told us to be content with food and clothing. How much more should we be content and thankful if we have more than food and clothing? Money is not evil. The root of evil is the love of money (see verse 10). When you become rich because of your love of money, which happens often for unbelievers, that's not the kingdom rich I am talking about in this book.

We can be rich and should be rich, but it has to be kingdom rich. We should be content no matter how much we have, even if we only have food and clothing. When we are at this contentment level, we have no attachment to money, and we won't fall into the trap of the love of money. Then we can have so much freedom and love to give and bless people. That's what God our Father does, and it's what He wants us to do, kingdom rich.

Some people might say we should not desire to be rich, according to verse 9: "Those who desire to be rich fall into temptation, into a snare…." But again, we need to read the Bible in context. This is referring to those who want to be rich for their own gain, not for God's will. When we do that, we are out of God's will and we would be like worldly people who only care about making money without minding our Father's business. The type of rich they crave is not kingdom rich. It's out of their own desire or lust for money. Therefore verse 10 says the root of evil is the love of money, not the money itself. In another words, the root of evil is the love for being rich, which is a type of lust. Being rich, on the other hand, is not evil. Kingdom rich is originated, developed and sustained by God and for God's kingdom's advancement.

Do you know when we are born again, we are born again rich? When we are born again, we are born into God's family and our Father is rich. We have been made heirs of everything, including physical riches from our rich, heavenly Father. When we are born again it is the end of our poverty. We can always go to the Source and have our needs met by our rich, heavenly Father according to His promise to us.

Misconception 2: God will provide, and I'll just wait and see Him come through.

This is a passive view of living. Yes, God provides, but money doesn't just fall on us. There are conditions for His provision. He definitely doesn't bless the lazy and the passive.

Whoever works his land will have plenty of bread, but he who follows worthless pursuits will have plenty of poverty. (Proverbs 28:19)

Diligence is emphasized in Proverbs for becoming rich.

For even when we were with you, we would give you this command: If anyone is not willing to work, let him not eat. (2 Thessalonians 3:10)

Paul said clearly here if someone is not willing to work, he shouldn't even eat. If you want to have plenty of bread to eat, you need to work your land. Time and opportunity are given to everyone equally. There is no accident in becoming rich or poor. How you end is more important than how you begin. Not everyone is born rich, but everyone can make a difference in life and have a big impact on others.

Religion that is pure and undefiled before God the Father is this: to visit orphans and widows in their affliction, and to keep oneself unstained from the world. (James 1:27)

There are needs all around us. God commanded us to take care of the poor, orphans, and widows.

If we are poor, or if we simply don't have more than enough, how can we take good care of them? If not us, who will? It's our job to follow through with this command by being the head, not the tail, in our finances, so we can do good works for the Father.

Misconception 3: I can curse the rich.

Some people have a sour attitude towards the rich. If a believer is rich, they have an even bigger problem with that person. They think believers are not supposed to be rich, or that they should not own anything, let alone nice things. But the Bible teaches not to curse the rich.

Even in your thoughts, do not curse the king, nor in your bedroom curse the rich, for a bird of the air will carry your voice, or some winged creature tell the matter. (Ecclesiastes 10:20)

When people curse or revile the rich, it's either because they don't have the right view about being kingdom rich or they are jealous. In either case, if the person becomes rich, like the person he had a problem with, he wouldn't curse himself as a rich person. He would be totally OK with it. That is not from God.

A tranquil heart gives life to the flesh, but envy makes the bones rot. (Proverbs 14:30)

Misconception 4: when we become rich, we made it; we've arrived.

This is absolutely wrong. We need to be kingdom rich. But that is not the ultimate goal in life. As a matter of fact, if we make being rich our ultimate goal, the riches we gain will not make us truly kingdom rich. There are many layers of prosperity in God's kingdom. Financial riches are a low level of prosperity in God's kingdom. As Proverbs says:

A good name is to be chosen rather than great riches, and favor is better than silver or gold. (Proverbs 22:1)

Jesus commanded this:

And he said to them, "Go into all the world and proclaim the gospel to the whole creation. (Mark 16:15)

Being kingdom rich is a way to facilitate this mission and fulfill the goal. It is not the goal.

Misconception 5: Jesus and Apostles in the Bible were poor. Therefore, God forbids us from being rich.

People who have this opinion often quote the following verses, and I'll discuss each one with you.

…as sorrowful, yet always rejoicing; as poor, yet making many rich; as having nothing, yet possessing everything. (2 Corinthians 6:10)

Because this verse, people say the early apostles were poor. We should be poor too. They ignore the latter part. It says: "…yet making many rich; as having nothing, yet possessing everything." Early apostles gave up their secular careers for the sake of preaching the Gospel. They lived on people's giving/donations for the most part, according to 1

Corinthians 9:6-14. By preaching and teaching, they made their followers rich in every way. If someone says "rich" here doesn't include material riches, they have no Biblical backing.

Another part of the Bible people use to oppose being rich is Acts 3:1-8:

Now Peter and John were going up to the temple at the hour of prayer, the ninth hour. 2 And a man lame from birth was being carried, whom they laid daily at the gate of the temple that is called the Beautiful Gate to ask alms of those entering the temple. 3 Seeing Peter and John about to go into the temple, he asked to receive alms. 4 And Peter directed his gaze at him, as did John, and said, "Look at us." 5 And he fixed his attention on them, expecting to receive something from them. 6 But Peter said, "I have no silver and gold, but what I do have I give to you. In the name of Jesus Christ of Nazareth, rise up and walk!" 7 And he took him by the right hand and raised him up, and immediately his feet and ankles were made strong. 8 And leaping up, he stood and began to walk, and entered the temple with them, walking and leaping and praising God. (Acts 3:1-8)

People mention that Peter said in verse 6, "I have no silver and gold." "They didn't possess silver and gold, so we shouldn't either," they reason. But Peter didn't say, "We never have money."

Have you ever gone out without any cash? Have you seen a beggar and wanted to give him some cash, and then you realize you don't have any? Just by looking at this one verse and discarding all other truths related to riches in the Bible is dangerous. As is developing a theory that they were poor, and that therefore we as modern believers ought not to be rich.

Just one chapter after this glorious record of healing, the Bible records something equally glorious about the early Church's financial status:

Now the full number of those who believed were of one heart and soul, and no one said that any of the things that belonged to him was his own, but they had everything in common. 33 And with great power the apostles were giving their testimony to the resurrection of the Lord Jesus, and great grace was upon them

all. 34 There was not a needy person among them, for as many as were owners of lands or houses sold them and brought the proceeds of what was sold 35 and laid it at the apostles' feet, and it was distributed to each as any had need. (Acts 4:32-36)

Verse 34 says there was not a needy person among them. That included Peter and John who said in chapter 3 they had no silver and gold! The money, which in today's terms would amount to millions of dollars, was laid at their feet.

Matthew 8:20 is also another verse people use to oppose believers being rich. Let me quote from verse 18 to 20:

Now when Jesus saw a crowd around him, he gave orders to go over to the other side. 19 And a scribe came up and said to him, "Teacher, I will follow you wherever you go." 20 And Jesus said to him, "Foxes have holes, and birds of the air have nests, but the Son of Man has nowhere to lay his head."

As I mentioned earlier, when we read the Bible, we need to see a big picture. It is very dangerous to take one section of the Bible and develop a theory out of it, then disregard the rest of the related verses which say the exact opposite of our theory. Read and understand the Word of God in context.

When Jesus said in verse 20 that the Son of Man has nowhere to lay His head, he was telling the scribe that he must preach the Good News of the kingdom of God.

As Luke 4:42-43 says:

And when it was day, he departed and went into a desolate place. And the people sought him and came to him, and would have kept him from leaving them, 43 but he said to them, "I must preach the good news of the kingdom of God to the other towns as well; for I was sent for this purpose." (Luke 4:42-43)

So Jesus had to be mobile. He was telling the scribe that his life may not be as glamorous as the scribe thought. When we preach the Gospel around the world, we don't get to stay at 5-star hotels every time, let alone being able to lay your head on your own bed every night. In this regard, foxes and birds have a better situation. It has nothing to do with us being poor or rich.

Another frequently quoted verse people use to say Jesus was poor is in Luke 2:7:

And she gave birth to her firstborn son and wrapped him in swaddling cloths and laid him in a manger, because there was no place for them in the inn. (Luke 2:7)

They say Jesus was born in a manger. Therefore, he was poor. But if we read this verse carefully without preconception, we can see clearly that Mary gave birth to Jesus in a manger not because they were poor, but because there was no place for them in the inn. The inn was full. A baby was coming. She did what she had to do at that moment.

In Matthew 2:10-11:

When they saw the star, they rejoiced exceedingly with great joy. 11 And going into the house, they saw the child with Mary his mother, and they fell down and worshiped him. Then, opening their treasures, they offered him gifts, gold and frankincense and myrrh. (Matthew 2:10-11)

The Magi saw baby Jesus and they fell down and worshiped him. Then the Word says, "opening their treasures, they offered Him gifts, gold and frankincense and myrrh." They didn't just give the baby onesies or PJs. Those gifts were treasures, expensive gifts, because wise men recognized and knew that this baby is the King of kings. He was not an ordinary baby. He was born from heavenly royalty. He was born rich. Offering Him gifts was the wise men's way to honor the King and the Savior.

And a ruler asked him, "Good Teacher, what must I do to inherit eternal life?" 19 And Jesus said to him, "Why do you call me good? No one is good except God alone. 20 You know the commandments: 'Do not commit adultery, Do not murder, Do not steal, Do not bear false witness, Honor your father and mother.'" 21 And he said, "All these I have kept from my youth."

22 When Jesus heard this, he said to him, "One thing you still lack. Sell all that you have and distribute to the poor, and you will have treasure in heaven; and come, follow me." 23 But when he heard these things, he became very sad, for he was extremely rich. 24 Jesus, seeing that he had become sad, said, "How difficult it is for those who have wealth to enter the kingdom of God! 25 For it is easier for a camel to go through the eye of a needle than for a rich person to enter the kingdom of God." 26 Those who heard it said, "Then who can be saved?" 27 But he said, "What is impossible with man is possible with God." 28 And Peter said, "See, we have left our homes and followed you." 29 And he said to them, "Truly, I say to you, there is no one who has left house or wife or brothers or parents or children, for the sake of the kingdom of God, 30 who will not receive many times more in this time, and in the age to come eternal life." (Luke 18:18-30)

Sometimes people quote verses 24-25 to say being rich is not right. The idea is, "Being rich stops a person from entering into the kingdom of God." But again, if you read these verses carefully, without traditional, religious glasses, you can see that Jesus said in verse 27, "What is impossible with man is possible with God." He was not saying it was impossible for the rich to enter into the kingdom of God. He was saying it can be hard for them because rich people tend to put their trust in their riches, if they don't know God.

But if a rich person follows God, he wouldn't fall into the trap of the love of money, just like many great rich leaders' examples in the Bible, quoted earlier in this book. He never said we should never be rich. We should be rich and, at the same time, we are supposed to give up everything to follow God. And this is possible and doable through God. When we have no attachment to money, we won't fall into the trap of the love of money. We will be free to give and free to bless. That's freedom! Praise our heavenly Father; it is totally possible.

Chapter 9
Closing Words

May you be blessed by the LORD, who made heaven and earth! 16 The heavens are the LORD's heavens, but the earth he has given to the children of man. (Psalm 115:15-16)

The reward for humility and fear of the LORD is riches and honor and life. (Proverbs 22:4)

God gave the earth to the children of man—that's us. We are called to rule on this earth as a governing assembly. Let's strive to walk into the fullness of what God has for us in every way, including in our personal finances, to fulfill God's callings in our lives.

Let the humility and fear of the Lord be put on us all the time. So we will be rewarded with riches and honor and life. Reign with Jesus on this earth before He returns!

My favorite figure who exemplifies kingdom rich is Job, who was regarded in God's eyes as a blameless and upright man, and there was none like him on earth. Yet he was the wealthiest of all the people of the east, living his life for God.

Let us learn from and imitate the heroes in the Bible, so that we can be modern Abrahams, Isaacs, Josephs and Jobs for our families, cities and nations because we are meant to be a blessing to our world. We are meant to be the solutions for nations!

Recommended Resources

Other Books by Sonia O'Brien
- 25 Words

By David O'Brien
- For Freedom
- Shine
- The Corinthian Mysteries
- Return to Acts Christianity
- Heal the Sick
- Jesus The King (Evangelistic)

By Apostle Charles Ndifon (PSOM.org)
- Kingdom Business Institute
- The Power School of Miracles (biannual event)
- Other books, audio and video material

www.BlueDiamondBookhouse.com

We welcome your positive feedback!!

If you'd like to send us a positive comment, please send a video or written **TESTIMONIAL** to us. Include your name, where you're from and briefly how this book enhanced your life:

BlueDiamondBookhouse.com

Thank you!

Made in the USA
Columbia, SC
15 October 2022